Athletes wi

by Cushla Brown

Focus Points

Disabilities

What are these athletes doing?

What is this athlete doing?

What is this athlete doing?

1.81
METRES
Check
Water Depth
2

What are these athletes doing?

What is this athlete doing?

What are these athletes doing?

14
13
12
11

What is this athlete doing?

What is this athlete doing?